EYE

Sati Mookherjee

Copyright©2022 Sati Mookherjee

ISBN: 978-1-7369169-3-3
LCCN: 2022931972

FIRST EDITION

Published by
Ravenna Press

ravennapress.com

for *Dadun*

Sri Anil Hari Chatterjee

1908 - 2001

Contents

KAL   *1*
Bellingham

DUKKHO   *5*
Jaynagar – Kolkata – Manchester – Copenhagen – London

KAL   *47*
Seattle – Kolkata – Bellingham

Author's Note

In Bengali
Dukkho, from the Sanskrit, means "Sorrow"
Kal means "Yesterday," "Tomorrow"

KAL

The eye is the first circle; the horizon which it forms is the second.... It is the highest emblem in the cipher of the world.

-Ralph Waldo Emerson, "Circles"

In my childhood home was a globe of the moon,
muddied celadon, with the ancient magma oceans

just as they look from earth: *Serenitiatis. Nubium.*
I'd turn the globe this way and that: ahead, back,

slow, fast. Trace the fine blue scribbles that meant *height*,
the brims of basins, where blunt mountains lapped.

And wonder, then, at how someone reasonable and smart
had marked lines of latitude and longitude—

fixed a lunar Orient, a West.
Wonder at how the white fields and grey fields blanched

and shaded the moon's face into cartoons
of rabbit and man. Years later I studied

the moon's mantle and crust, the colorless grit of spinel,
feldspar. Examined photographs: an orange, I thought:

newly peeled, spoked with strings of pith. And looked closer still,
at the chemical signatures of comets, their glancing

paths. The ceaseless rain of meteor impacts.
Of solar winds, raking grains of solar dust

into the moon's native soil. I learned to read
what that polished globe spinning under my hand

(tomorrow / yesterday / tomorrow) told:
a story of travelers and immigrants.

DUKKHO

Have other eyes, new light!
And look!

-Bhagavad Gita, Chapter 11

1.

In the summer of 1932, the season Varsha, my grandfather wrote,
I rose early one morning. It was still cool. A moon went stale

in the western sky. The courtyard pigeons shifted
in their nests, sleep thinned by the blade of light slipping

down the brick. I think of him there, at a shadow-shot desk, idly
batting the peeling globe with his fingertips

until the revolutions effaced every ocean and continent.
I took a last meal in my sister's home. A swallow

of milk somersaulted twice in the teacup
and succumbed. He was only twenty-three, convicted

of sedition, conspiracy against the Crown.
Twice imprisoned. Unrepentent.

So the Raj devised new punishment,
at once terrible and inglorious: banishment

to Manchester, England, belly of the beast.
Quit India indeed.

The train shuddered, waiting.
On the little finger of his right hand, a ring

—honey cat's-eye—prescribed
for insight, for perception,

as protection against drowning.
And with three steep steps,

my grandfather climbed into exile.

2.

The express train lilting and
lurching went parting
the plains. He bid a careful farewell
to the flatlands, tiled in paddy and field
in shades from mustard to emerald.
And invoked what he could not see:

the cleft mountains of the north, pasted with glaciers.
The temple of the goddess at the southern tip,
where three oceans—indigo, green, cinnamon—met.
This world would sustain

he reminded himself, when he left,
if ever he returned and if he didn't, he had only
to close his eyes to come home to it.

He had a tiffin of coconut sweets
and peppered potato curry,
but did not eat, only looked out
between the soot-crusted rails until dusk filled
in everything, then leaned his head back
and shut his eyes until he felt certain that first all of it,
then none of it, belonged to him.

3.

All that night he walked
the terraced shores of Kashi,

sandals sounding a counter-
time to his heartbeat, polishing the image

of his father's face in his mind
like a stone. The air was congested

with the peregrine souls of the dead,
the alleys long emptied of mourners and yogis,

the funeral pyres unflamed.
Only the *Dom* were out, to scrub the burning grounds,

and they were as the dead: Invisible. Nomads. Casteless.
Their song lavish in the night: *You, third petal*

of a green flower The murky light of butter lamps
mottled my grandfather's path with shadow.

The moon in diaspora.
The sky vacant.

4.

The country settled. By day it had whirled about him,
stirred by wheels, by the soles of tribals
dragging wagons and dust-clouds and squinting cloud-
colored goats: *Asuras*. The *Gaddi*. *Gadia Lohar*,

in boat-shaped carts. The Kashmiri *Gujjar*.
Sarania, sword-sharpeners. Copper-smelting *Kasars*.
Dhadi, geneologists and bards. They cleaved

to ancient paths, over clay and sand, through winds with names
and winds anonymous, cart-flanks ornamented with rice paste,
the spines of their donkeys painted mauve. *Home*
an always-young and always-dying thing:

the ebbing shade of a date tree in sun, or a low mud wall
snaking over the ground, taking its tail in its mouth
to make *place*—left, then, erased

with the next rain. The *Banjara* prayed
before a pack saddle when breaking camp;
as the tribe walked on, the goddess *Banjari Devi* sprang
from the saddle to the head of one of the cattle, sat rocking
in the parenthesis of its horns. My grandfather knew

of the restless circulation of these his countrymen,
as much as he knew of the currents of lymph or blood
under his skin, which is to say, next to nothing.
And all the while, over all their heads,

the domed sky turned about the hub of sun.

5.

The steamer pulled out of the harbor
at Bombay. His gut seized.
Evening: the conch shells lowed

over the soft pastures of his childhood village,
over the paths that led home, creased
with ruts that rainfall glazed silver,

palash flowers blazing
by the side of the road
even as night fell

even as the pickled tamarind melted
on his tongue, the puckered pit
rocky in his mouth
long after the sweet, salty flesh was gone

and, in the gathering dusk,
a falling sun smeared the low clouds vermilion,
rouged the temple's white body.

He kept the cratered stone buried
a while under his tongue:
toy moon, persistent

in his body's own darkness, persistent
in the abundant darkness of the larger world.

6.

The days were identical,
but the sea seemed
to change. Tumid, on rainy
afternoons, brimming.
In the ginger light of dawn,
when first he woke
it lay flat and velvet-shiny.
Sometimes a wind blew
out of nowhere, raising a nap
on the sleek. Once:
the horizon finely scored,

a hatch blackening
as the storm approached.
Then there it was:
the shadow of the plaqued clouds
riding the waves,
the rain falling straight down.
He held his arms out to it,
it rained upon his fingertips,
then his palms,
then his wrists. And stopped.
The ship pulled him away.
The rain stayed.

Nights, he sat on deck
thinking how eerily deep
was this sea that bore him.
Looked to the seeded sky,
lodestar, constellation, lost
to his eye. Recited Vedic verses aloud.

Sometimes the sea was a petrous thing
and the ship embedded.
Sometimes the boat stood still
and the sea washed over it
just as the sky streamed over
the balsa strake of moon.
For all its hues, he saw,
for all its shifting
bones and molting skins,
it was all the same—looking behind or ahead—

all tenses conjugated
to the present, this
the sea's wild talent.

7.

He was already practiced in grief, schooled
in the saddest of partings: his mother's death.
Since infancy had known an incomplete
world, lived at a perpetual precipice,

grief a perennial specimen
that minded an erratic season: blooming
and shuttering, blooming
again, its rare beauty more vivid

now that he was triply orphaned:
bereft of mother, motherland, and now

fatherless. Grandmother had been mother
to him, and *Durga* also mother
—but immortal, and perfect—

the boyhood festivals of the goddess
colored with an acute grace; he sought and found

tenderness in everything —the boisterous pageantry—
drums, gongs—and the beauty—
three hundred butter lamps

studded the path to his home, streamed down the path
to the river, gilding the meager current.
He loved best the preparations
in the days before, ordinary things turned holy.

Would linger at the thresholds
of the rooms where the women worked,

rolling cotton wicks between their fingers,
rubbing fragrant paste out of sandalwood pestle and mortar.

At five, he'd never been out of his village
with its infinite palette of greens: leaf, parrot, citrine.
Even stone succumbed to verdigris: a fine moss

seeped over the outer walls of the old homes. School
was the country he longed to explore.
The older boys strutted off every morning
and afternoon, leaving him to a lonely play, unpeopled.

Once he had been to the eastern edge of the village
where he was told night-dwelling spirits rose out of the far swamps,
played tag in the betel woods. He'd looked and looked

but could not summon a single ghost,
the horizon—ragged with the shaggy heads
of date-palms—unremarkable.

8.

His schoolhouse had eight thatch roofs
and no walls, soot-water for ink, scraped
toddy palm leaf for paper. The schoolmaster cupped
his hand around my grandfather's
to coax the vowels
from the sharpened bamboo slip of his pen.

He stood with the other boys
to sing the counting poem
his father had sung, and his father
before him, reconvening the ordinary world
in parts, from one to one hundred:

>*One moon,*

>*A fortnight in two weeks,*

>*Eyes in threes ...*

9.

The sea-sun meandered inland, paler
and more blond, and a new dream eclipsed
the last. To think one sky roofed

both lives, one blue-white slip
swaddling the world: originating here,
at the dirty city's far edge, and tucked in *there*,

past the green waters of the village pond,
just beyond the buckled mangroves.

He rose early to pray, those rites affording
a deeper rest than did sleep.
Poured a thumb-tip of Ganga water
into a brass bowl, traced a figure in the air,
transforming the water,

then sipped from the bowl, swallowed
and knew himself transformed.
Recited the *Gayatri* one hundred and eight times,

ancient petition for illumination, insight.
Dressed, then, in Western dress, stepped out, to walk,
tailing the milkfloat, or the costermonger's barrows

to market, where porters bore sacks of whelks
on their heads, heaved herring-stuffed cades,

he stayed, watched the market animate, the alleys
turning slick with fishgut and petals of scale. In Kashi

he had knelt at the river-slick step
to fill a medicine bottle at the clear fold of the Ganga—now,
only a month later,

the crescent sank
in the brown glass, and this diminishment panicked him.

He began to avert his gaze
when he took out the bottle from his trunk
and when he put it back. He did not weep,
did not remember when last he had wept,

his eyes were stones in his head.
He walked from market

to university, past the park—mothers
pushing prams, pigeons garbling in the coppiced trees—
such tidy trees.
He saw the screw palm on his childhood lane

ensnared in monsoon winds: disarrayed,
unable to wrench free, its serrated
silhouette, its wretched, rooted flailing.

10.

Sometimes the blind man had stood beneath that very palm,
the bulky harmonium around his neck bowing him,

its ivory keys splintering—his small son sang hymns
for alms in a sweet, nasal voice, sang of *Durga*,

of her consort, of the crescent moon snared in Shiva's
matted hair. Sometimes the traveling monkey-player

rested in its shade, macaques costumed
as spangled bride and groom, sometimes

the tin peddler, or the ash-blackened *sadhu*, in one year
the pregnant widow—returning the next winter

with a child at her breast, in the years next
the boy running ahead of her. How

he envied that child, ever-girded in original circumference:
the mother at his back, her gaze elastic

as the horizon, fast as
the seam of sky and sea.

11.

What language did these people speak?
not the English of his eight-roofed school,
not that of Bernard Shaw, or Shelley—*Please?*
he asked, or *Again?* so often
that one day both words sloughed their shells
and became pure sound, he couldn't remember what they meant,

and he was lost, homeless, a phantom
ignorance, immaterial as the bluish aura sleeving
a candle flame. Even the rain

felt foreign to him—unlike the glassy species he knew,
that made stream of street, turned footpath to spit,
this only dribbled, or was more insidious still,

stung the cheek a bit, plinked pores over the skin
of whatever lay stagnant. He'd walk home
along infinite row houses studded with flues
like dull little teeth, as though he lolled

in the mandible of some thick beast, was greeted thusly
by landlady Morris: *Meat, tea, luv, or sweet?* Her redded stoop!

the mutton thrice-salted! in her parlor, the eroding thoraces
of butterflies morgued in dusty cases.
My grandfather busied himself

with pharmacopeia and formulary, chemistry
another acquired tongue—with its immutable syntax
of elements and valences—and its simple diction ... watch glass,
beaker, the crucible in porcelain.
What was the bench but another altar,
where he effected alteration: annulment
and generation, he was a juggler,

the atoms jigging through his hands,
each a globe if he could have only seen it,
each a world unto itself, why, he was Atlas,
he was a priest, the languages of proof and prayer

sounding an identical acknowledgment:
the ongoing transformation of every substance.

12.

Among his jailers he learned
how a free people lived. And so the island
grew slighter by the day

until at last he patched his satchel,
jumped the strait: holiday.

He trekked the continent: woodlands,
and fringing windbreaks, dog's mercury and primrose,
bony stone walls edged with gorse,
ruddy fields of grain, under filmy skies
and skies that put stained glass to shame,

past medieval village churches,
their chinked, copped heads,
past bell towers messy with kestrel's nests.

    Veni, he wrote grandly, *vidi* ....

In Copenhagen he was the only man on foot,
the bicycles sped by, dizzying in their wake.
My grandfather rested against the Round Tower
where Tycho Brahe had charted

the stars as they rose,
regarded the roving moon:

Brahe's gaze so potent, it conquered

the very firmament, releasing
every planet and a full thousand stars
from the shells in which they had been confined,

broadcast them to undulant fathoms of sky.

13.

Oh, austere universe ...

His native astronomy teemed
with deities and divine beings,
all fattened on the nectar of the primordial milk-sea,

even the two invisible planets, Ketu and Rahu,

tail and head of a skulking beast that preyed
upon the moon and sun. In his boyhood
he had caught the sun in a pot
of pigmented water, watched the creeping creature fall upon it

about him the morning hour collapsed to dusk ....

Lunar path and solar path,
the professor intoned a decade later,
drawing across the vast black of the chalkboard
orbits limp as abandoned rosaries
beaded with planets and moons, *X's*

for *lunar* and *solar nodes: The two points in space
at which eclipses occur*

… then the sun passed out of the killing jaws,
and a vast light suffused the earthen bowl,
colored the air,

    Conjunction and opposition,

intimacy and separation,

his native astronomy had taught him
a cosmos in which will existed
independent of matter,

where intention was a force no less potent
for the absence of a host. The show over,
he tipped the bowl, and the deep blue sky,
holy sky, gushed out:

the soaked grass / his wet feet / what light still shone in the empty bowl

14.

He sought and found tenderness in everything,
located motherhood in any manifestation:

the fevered hummingbirds tending their nests in the deciduous wood,
Mrs. Morris's clumsy ministrations, Conrad's
Mary, kneeling at the foot of the cross.

He came to recast his exile
in a benevolence that irked his professor,
who stuffed his pipe's meerschaum bowl
in rough fury before replying: *Make no mistake,*

Britain is a tigress:
a gentle mother within her den, but beyond it,
predator and carnivore, nothing less.

But he was no stranger to mother-warriors,
reared by *Durga*, by *Kali*, by his own mother,
whom death had made omnipotent,
who existed unencumbered by body, as pure will:

a bird of prey brooding eggs hard as stone,
Mary keening in a stony field,
above her the son dying, but to live again.

15.

In the laboratory he folded circles
of filter paper into cones, decanted,
sucked acids into the glass stems of pipettes.
He created the clotted orange

precipitate of chinoidine,
and herapathite, amber as resin. Dribbled chlorine
in ammonia water until the beaker flashed jade,

until a body of clear bright needles appeared
in a bubbling beaker—then touched air and effloresced.

And he sketched these events—as all the C's and H's
and SO4's clasped electrons
and bonded and double-bonded—

he filled pages with hexagons and dashes, stylized lidless eyes
that observed the constant conversion of matter,
the perpetual transformation of substances.
One evening, in midst of some frothing experiment

he became aware of a low buzzing, a hornet dying
on the workbench, its deathspin
centrifuge-rapid. He could almost see

the clear pellet of soul spit out. This death overwhelmed him.
He put his head to the table and wept. In the window

a blue wagon, painted with scallops and scrolls—Travellers—
crossed the pasture. The dray horse stepped carefully
along the old ruts left by other caravans,
the sunken, delible scars of movement.

16.

Toward a geography of self—in the bath he surveyed
his body: the interrupting islands—*knee* and *knee*—
the inclining *chest* a kind of continental shelf,
bathwater configured in channels and straits about him,
the banks white as Dover's, and within him

a correspondent landscape,
that would manifest were he to dissolve,
and internal and external become confluent—
as in death, as in the dissolution wrought
by dreams—in any place time was a stagnant
sort of thing that ran nowhere,

was a whorled, containing sea that collected
various embedded topographies.... And what if he

were to tip his *head* back for a moment—just so—
enough to catch a sliver-view of flocculent sky
through the leaded window,
there the mossy overhang of eave,
what if he were to draw the proverbial veil,
inch down the porcelain cliff, submit to the heat, sleep
—but alas! the cake of soap flung itself in

with a rousing splash, he flailed, chased cloud and film
until *hand* emerged in victory out of the churning milk-sea,
and, renegade restored to its tub's edge perch, he settled,
blew *palm* free of froth … the bubbles drifted to the open window,
but for one that lingered, did not want to leave—hovered

before his face—in the slippery lens his own eye, staring—
then it rose, nimbly floating across the sill, dragging his reflection into
the world,
he watched it continue up the street, until, at its peak
it was only *figure*, a hollow body—

so he willed it, then, his traveling eye,
across the curvature of the sky, whisked it over sea
and continent, through time,

all the way home to the massive spine of the Himalaya,
where, fortified in the ice-air, everything potential
rendered kinetic, he raced downgrade

over terraced fields, over the spangled Buddhist temples
of Sikkim, over hill stations, gardens of tea,
over Mungpoo (where a bungalow awaited him,
and the air held his children)—
he journeyed still, down the coast:
tungsten mines, forests of cinchona and teak,
limestone laced with lines of ruby like arteries, turned

finally over the Bay of Bengal—arrested
there above the delta-striped shore, the alluvial mouth
of the whirled, containing sea, its dimpling eddies,
over muddy shoals jumpy
with fish and littered with dinghies,
where the mirrored clouds
ride long, long waves that arrived, touched shore and ceased to be.

17.

He had always revered his father's face in repose,
wondered, with a child's generous reason,
whether the human soul deserted
the sleeping body—was it skittish

as a butterfly? could it be reined, by will?
like the dragonflies he leashed with thread
and flew about his head in circles....

The tides of his breath
scarcely stirred his father's body.
Two mynahs squabbled at the window.
The shutter squeaked. Pressed
against his father on the high teak bed,

he looked into his face, then let his focus
blur, until, between his father's two eyes
there appeared a third—

it lingered
just above the bridge of his nose,
until the effort became too great—

he blinked
it away, turned to watch the slip of cloth
at the window fill and empty
of its own accord, until his father awoke,

and somewhere, in a thorough darkness,
a butterfly alit, folded its clear wing.

18.

On a clear Saturday in Manchester,
in the lap of the park bench, jumper
for pillow he napped, dreaming in the profuse light of noon,
the richness of that light
recalling the ancient Pali prayer: *the sun is like an eye*

shining brilliantly down—but what of the marketing
put off, *I must buy my supper's bread*, he thought,
then two-stepped from *bread* to *beget*,
glided idly to *bereft*—ah! the sharp flower opening
in his chest—but *bring me a mustard seed
from a home that has not known death*, a Hindu prince
commanded a grieving woman, it was said,

and the beggar widow's son, there under the screw-palm
—what became of him? Schoolmaster? Tailor?
my grandfather placed a needle in his hand, but it elongated,
crisscrossed into a plow-line

and the widow's son stood upon a dirt dike that ran haphazard
over the fertile land of Bengal like a scar,
black water-buffalo lunging chest-deep through the paddy at his feet
—does he see his own perfect reflection

in the hazy water, twin halves of a hinge—man, animal: animal, man
—does his stance at prayer mirror his father's?

does the mother hear the husband's voice soar
out of the throat of the chanting son?—*Durga   Durga   Durga!*

The prayer beads tumble through his fingers,
the great soundless Bengal sky opens up—
dark-bellied cumuli whorled as fingerprints,
a great wind uncoiling, the air suddenly black,

my grandfather shivered, though he lay in profuse sunlight
on the lap of a bench, in a park, jumper for pillow,
marketing put off, on a clear Saturday in Manchester.

19.

When the stone fell out of his ring,
it was Mrs. Morris who recovered it,
on the second day of its absence,
there behind the foot of his bed
—*Why, a chrysoberyl! Come,
I will show you a marvelous thing!* she said.
She drew the drapes, held a flashlight at a slant
and turned the stone beneath it:
half-spheres of milk and shadow rolled
in perfect eclipses across the stone's surface.
The light did not waver in her hand,
a toy sun, an eye shining brilliantly down.
Mrs. Morris looked upon the stone,
and he knew her face: it was the face of his father
at prayer, it was his own gaze,
at the laboratory bench, agent
of his every prayer,
instrument of acknowledgment.

20.

Before the hearth a fire sank
too dim to read by. Sighing,

he reached for the lamp
to illumine the page,
and that new light fell fractured,

in soft shavings about a solid core.
It shone upon his prayer book,

upon the face of *Durga*.
The light gathered
in a corona about her head, transforming her

into a Mary painted in oils, haloed,
or pieced in colored glass in a church window.

He stared
at the hybrid God he had made.

Then turned off the light, seeking
darkness, remembering
the fragrant prayer room of his childhood home,

and how the women had knelt there, consecrating

flower, fruit, a folded cloth
with their attention.

21.

For months my grandfather had held his grief
at arm's length, until one day he woke, and found:

he could contain it, or it contained him—

it eddied about him, atmospheric, it was an ocean,
an eerily deep sea that bore him.

He returned to museums and churches
he had already visited, looked again at the *pietas*:

a mother, a son, and a finite grief.
Read the *Bhagavad Gita*,
and the Sanskrit sounded all day long in his head:

> *And eyes,—on every side*
> *Perfect, diversified;*
> *And nowhere end of Thee, nowhere beginning*

He poured the rest of the Ganga water
with a great splash into his prayer bowl

and his next time in London

rinsed out the bottle at the shore of the Thames,
then held it just below

the water's skin. The bottle, filling,
jittered and bucked in his hand like a living thing.

22.

I have a photograph of him, taken somewhere on the Continent,
his back unshaped by a knapsack,

bulky boots on his feet, his left hand lost in his pocket, and I shut my eyes
to see the cat's eye ring on the little finger—prescribed for insight, perception

and protection against drowning. He was allowed to return
home after seven years, in 1939

when England entered the war. Had booked a berth on a cargo ship
but arrived in Liverpool late,

to the sight of the placid horizon, the departed boat.
The next night a German raider

met the ship, and sank her.
I recall that photograph: a tawny sky, some thin trees.

Behind those, moor, lea, heath … jungle, paddy.
My grandfather prayed every night to dream his father,

because there was a precision in the dreaming
that was not possible by day, when he found he could not recollect

his face, not *exactly*. And this grief was deepest.
How hopefully he would arrive at sleep. It was a ritual dear as any,

the glad renunciation of world, of body, only the eye left
to lurch about in the socket, conjuring.

KAL

... arranged so, earth held up between such satellites as *sun*, as *eye*....

-Richard Kenney, "The Invention of the Zero"

1.

The vowel of wind turns over in the flue.

All week the sky was gluey with clouds, last night
dark bolls sat sodden on the rising moon,

molding it as if it were pulp too. But now
the scratch of the chestnut's leathery leaves against glass,
and I raise the blinds to find the grain-tipped weeds

bowing their braided heads, the matted cloud
lifting in layers like a feline eyelid, and there it is:
still lit, pied by crater and *mare*.

Such stillness at this velocity—we're whisked along
and feel nothing of it. A plodding moon
above the shed. Somewhere behind us,

a sun, combusting. Lunar eclipse tonight—
soon three bodies will stage a moment unlike
and like any other. How quietly

it will all transpire: a kind of virtuosity.

In this room my smallest work makes noise.
So the burner ticks as the pot of water heats; cream plashes

in the pan. And the knot of garlic yields
perfect gibbous cloves,
but not before they've skidded over the counter, rained
a petite rain onto the linoleum.

First contact: the moon in penumbra,
shadow-sleeved, shaded

almost imperceptibly.

2.

I finish cooking while my infant son sleeps.
With two threads of saffron
a bronze flush ruddies the cream.
Light from the window drapes

the dark patio, the potted maple sapling,
its broadcast shadow a constellation
of aberrant stars. A northwest
pacific. Something stirs
the bramble—cedar waxwings come downhill.

Hooded gulls have returned
to Bengal's bay from the alluvial shores
of Tibetan lakes, wailing, singing.
What forces have colluded to pull them there

or to pull this child to me.
What histories of loss and migration, leave-taking,

the overlapping orbits of the exiled, the immigrant, the refugee.

This ringed earth, jangling with longitude,
hoops of magnetic force, currents, jet streams....

A mark of fine red dust on my fingertip.
A little wind kicks the screen.

3.

My daughter
is yet unborn, unconceived,

she hovers someplace
beyond the opaque atmosphere around me.

And I wonder
am I the satellite, or is she?

So I wait for the moment of the complete eclipse, of totality—
when she is pulled out of me, arched and bloody,

saturated in light,
and I am shadow so deep

I recede infinitely

4.

I have staged many an eclipse,
under my grandfather's tutelage.

On the lower roof of the Kolkata house
the washing dried above our heads.
On the highest line—from rebar
to potted jackfruit tree, his saffron-edged
prayer *dhuti* snapped in the breeze,
most splendid sail in an armada of ordinary.

Behind us, in the wire-fronted cage,
blue and green songbirds idled
in their terrible captivity.

A jackfruit, oblong, spiny, was the sun,
a *batabi* lemon, earth. The moon an orange.
We painted the fruit with rice paste
that by night dried to a white shell.
My grandfather held the flashlight.

I moved moon and earth. First contact.
Second contact. Totality. The jackfruit
(in its borrowed light) burned and burned.

5.

Afternoon worship.

Two years before his death,
I am at the threshold
of the shuttered room where my grandfather sits
within white walls of net.

Cello-taped to the pocked wall
a poster of the *Mother Durga*
garlanded in hibiscus.

Through one open shutter
a spray of magnesium light
from the welder's torch,

brilliant even in midday.
And in the sky a bird of prey,
a kite-hawk perhaps,

almost motionless, though a tremor at the wingtips betrays
the tension sustained by a body in stasis.

The prayer beads circling through his hand
at once fall and rise.

My gaze follows his, returns
to *Durga's* face, to her third eye, upright
as a spear of candle flame,

vanishing point.

The hawk drops out of the sky.
I shut my eyes

to see it
streak by, to complete the infinite arc of its flight.

6.

How the mind gambols, gambles,
on the surety, the buttresses, of memory.

I was three.

I sat on my mother's lap, in my lap a picture book.
She pointed to the first word.

I examined the rigid right angle,
the double orbs, the last letter
all akimbo—a kicking leg, a thrusting arm.
And read, before she could:

"Look."

My mother held her breath.
In my eye, she later recalled,
the pupil flared so wide
the iris slimmed to piping.

"Look!"

The fleeting half-life of that word—
one moment pluripotent, possible,
in the next, something cased
in a museum of apostrophes, fossil.

7.

As a child I'd lie
on the orange shag pile
of our ranch house den,

examine from that inverted angle
what hung on the walls,
the objects on the mantel—

a carved box, a jade apple,
the dusty underside
of its brittle leaf—

I'd take things apart
with my gaze: a canvas
of cornflowers in a vase

just a mess of streaks and clots
of paint. *Durga*
inked on brown silk,

third eye cradled
in a crescent-moon *teep*.

One afternoon, as my eyes glazed

in the moment before sleep,
my focus shifted
and that middle eye seemed

to lift off her face.
It hung between us

in the air

a window, a lens,
I looked through it
and then I dreamed.

8.

Two months to the day after his passing,
I read my grandfather's memoirs.

Of his own grandmother's death
he wrote: *At dawn we bathed her body*

in the river. I almost fainted
from a grief that seemed to weight

my every limb.
The Bengali script, in the pale blue ink

of his fountain pen, dripped from the ledger lines,
much as the roots of a banyan tree stream

from its outstretched branches. *I washed her face,*
I translated. *I thought I would shatter.*

9.

He who sees dukkha sees also

the arising of dukkha

sees also the cessation of dukkha

The tethered goat kicks up

its back heels, smelling

the chemical scent

of the coming storm,

the river turtle deepens the soil nest

around its quivering, leathery eggs,

upon a knotted-yarn mat

the Buddha sits, the rain begins.

and sees also the path

leading to cessation of dukkha

but that I have always found difficult to believe.

10.

The sky behind me was blue,
the clouds white,

and the sky ahead its perfect inverse: white
with periwinkle cumuli,

and overhead the line of transfer,
translucent. Over a high fence came

the voices of invisible children, a rubber ball
smacking cement. I saw

the stone of earth wrapped in such a sky,
thought of a life contained in time,

time not linear, not infinite, but continuous:
a cipher, a circling line,

summing all things
to a zero greater than its parts. One child cried out, then,

louder than the other boys
I could not tell, if in pain or in joy.

11.

My son and I
play catch on a brittle autumn night

beneath the shining porch light.

Three,
he shouts happily
every time he throws up the ball:

occluding the light, erasing himself from my sight
until the ball falls to rest in my hands.

Simple props: a rubber ball,
a circle of light, a child
replete with joy.

We stage the story again and again:
how once we stood, two travelers, each unseen to the other,
waiting—

until the circle of shadow fell away
to give me to him, and him to me.

12.

Totality: the moon blotted out
but for a hennaed ring.
I carry my grandfather's daughter's
daughter's son outside. His gaze drifts

over the cove of sky, but alights
on the moon—I know by the burnished rim of light
showing in his eye.

Our self-portrait, I tell him, in silhouette,
our own shadow cast:

the shadow of this ringed earth,
its remembered and forgotten histories, telescoping
futures, currents, passages, orbitals,

laments, laughter, bird songs.

The shadow of the sunken boat.

The shadow of the fork-tailed tern
hunting the waters off a Bengal beach.

The shadow of the Dom tribal's reed brush, freckled
with the ashes of the mourned and unmourned.

The shadow of my girl, still unformed.

And of this son, his eye so glossed
I can watch the eclipse in it—my own self
mirrored twice, married to *moon*, to *eye*

—and as I watch, the muscles of his iris tense
the black night of the pupil opening still more wide,
pulling the eclipsed moon in,

holding it, holding all of us, up to the sky.

Author's Note:

The excerpts from the *Bhagavad Gita* are from Sir Edwin Arnold's <u>The Song Celestial: A Poetic Version of the *Bhagavad Gita*</u>, first published in 1885.

The poems are loosely based on my grandfather's memoirs. Exiled by the Raj, he studied in Manchester, traveled the Continent, and ultimately returned safely to India (the ship he missed was in fact torpedoed). All embellishments are of course a poet's prerogative, if not duty. However, there is one dissonant note I must acknowledge —the chrysoberyl ring that I place on my grandfather's hand. My great-grandfather, Sri Rampada Chattopadhyay, born in 1872, was a philosopher and Vedantist. As such, neither he, nor his son, would have subscribed to cultural superstitions such as the attribution of protective powers to stones or amulets.

Interested readers may find Sri Rampada Chattopadyay's scholarship in English translation in <u>A Vaisnava Interpretation of the Brahmasutras: Vedanta and Theism</u> (1992, E.J. Brill).

Grateful acknowledgment is made to the Washington State Arts Commission and Artist Trust for both a Fellowship Award, and a Grant for Artists Projects (GAP) award, which made possible the completion of this work. I am thankful to the Multnomah County Library in Portland, Oregon, for a residency in the Sterling Room for Writers.

Earlier versions of the following poems appeared in <u>Jump Start: A Northwest Renaissance Anthology</u>: "Kal" (*In my childhood home …*) and "Kal # 11, as "Story" (*My son and I …*). In 2019, the manuscript for *Eye* was a finalist for the Gaudy Boy Prize sponsored by Singapore Unbound.

I am deeply grateful to Allen Braden, John Davis, Sharon Hashimoto, Susan Landgraf, Robert McNamara, Arlene Naganawa, Michael Spence, and Ann Spiers for their thoughtful critiques of this manuscript in its earlier incarnations.

Last, I am indebted to my mother, Supriya Mookherjee, for the game we played throughout my early childhood, in the car, in the kitchen ... *Let's paint word-pictures!*

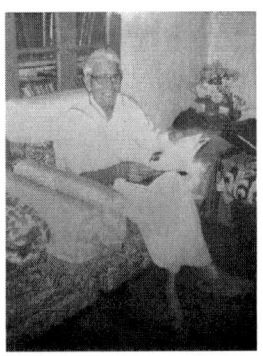

Sri Anil Hari Chattopadhyay, Kolkata 1995

Back cover photograph: Sri Anil Chattopadhyay, Mungoo 1965.
Author photograph: Hannah Feller.